INSPIRE
COMMUNITY

Inspire Christian Writers
EQUIPPING WRITERS TO INSPIRE THE WORLD

INSPIRE COMMUNITY

Inspiring Writings About the Power of Community

ANTHOLOGY 2021

Edited by
DEBRA CELOVSKY
and
ROBYNNE ELIZABETH MILLER

INSPIRE COMMUNITY

Copyright © 2021 Inspire Christian Writers. Individual pieces within this anthology are copyrights of the authors.

All rights reserved. No part of this publication may be reproduced, distributed, translated, or transmitted in any form or by any means, including photocopying, recording, or other electronic or mechanical methods, without the prior written permission of the author, except in the case of brief quotations embodied in critical reviews and certain other noncommercial uses permitted by copyright law.

ISBN 978-1-938196-20-1

Scripture quotations marked (ESV) are taken from The ESV® Bible (The Holy Bible, English Standard Version®), copyright © 2001 by Crossway, a publishing ministry of Good News Publishers. Used by permission. All rights reserved.

Scripture quotations marked (NASB) are taken from the (NASB®) New American Standard Bible®, Copyright © 1960, 1971, 1977, 1995, 2020 by The Lockman Foundation. Used by permission. All rights reserved. www.lockman.org

Scripture quotations marked (NIV) are taken from the Holy Bible, New International Version®, NIV®. Copyright © 1973, 1978, 1984, 2011 by Biblica, Inc.™ Used by permission of Zondervan. All rights reserved worldwide. www.zondervan.com. The "NIV" and "New International Version" are trademarks registered in the United States Patent and Trademark Office by Biblica, Inc.™

Scripture quotations marked (TCR/NIV) are taken from The Thompson Chain-Reference® Bible New International Version Copyright © 1983 by The B. B. Kirkbride Bible Company, Inc. and The Zondervan Corporation. The Holy Bible, New International Version Copyright © 1978 by New York International Bible Society.

Scripture quotations marked (NLT) are taken from the Holy Bible, New Living Translation, copyright ©1996, 2004, 2015 by Tyndale House Foundation. Used by permission of Tyndale House Publishers, Carol Stream, Illinois 60188. All rights reserved.

Scripture quotations marked (TLB) are taken from The Living Bible copyright © 1971. Used by permission of Tyndale House Publishers, Carol Stream, Illinois 60188. All rights reserved.

Cover designed by MiblArt
Interior design & layout by Author Digital Services
Published by Inspire Christian Writers

Dedication

This anthology is dedicated to all those who long for community. And to the writers of Inspire, who are not just friends and colleagues ... they're family.

> And let us consider how we may spur one another on toward love and good deeds, not giving up meeting together, as some are in the habit of doing, but encouraging one another — and all the more as you see the Day approaching. (Hebrews 10:24-25)

Special thanks to:

Debra Celovsky,
Robynne E. Miller,
Ian Feavearyear,
The entire editorial team
(boy, are you guys amazing!),
And the board of directors of
Inspire Christian Writers.
Without all of you, this project
would never have happened.

Thank you.

Contents

Introduction | 1

1 Blessed are the Peacemakers
by Christine Hagion 3

2 Creating a Community Care Group for Connection
by Deb Gruelle 11

3 Finding Contentment
by Marilyn Siden 19

4 Fitting In
by Susan Sage 25

5 Food for Thought
by D.H. Weinberg 31

6 A Heart for Community
by Christy Hoss 39

7 Indemic
by Terrie Hellard-Brown 47

8 Intentional Isolation
by Randy Brundage 51

9	Knowing They Are There by Malcolm Mackinnon	57
10	Lost in the Crowd by Debbie Jones Warren	61
11	Lydia by Debra Celovsky	69
12	The Murmuration of Community by Tessa Burns	77
13	My People by Robynne Elizabeth Miller	85
14	Saving Nineveh by Damon J. Gray	91
15	The Picture by Robynne Elizabeth Miller	99
16	We are Family by Ruth Ella Wilson	107
17	A Woman Leave Her Home by Robynne Elizabeth Miller	111

Index of Authors | 119
Meet the Authors | 121
About Inspire Christian Writers | 127

INSPIRE
COMMUNITY

Introduction

In the two years leading up to the publishing of this anthology, the world has been a bit upside-down. To use some typical British understatement, it's been a challenging couple of years.

In these years, we've learned to attend school differently, work differently, and even shop differently. Most of these changes meant some combination of computer screens, online meetings or classes, and hand sanitizer. It's been a little rough. Even for writers, who tend to be introverts as a whole.

In fact, so many opportunities for connection have been changed or canceled completely that we've had to dig deep to find ways to stay engaged with our friends, family, co-workers and, well, the entire world.

And that may be one of the few threads of silver lining that will remain when the world is free again to go about its business ... we have learned to be creative and intentional when it comes to maintaining community. Because we've had to push the pause button on our in-person relationships, we've been forced us to find other ways to connect.

And, we've done it.

Zoom meetings. Online school. Drive-by birthday parties. Socially distanced playdates.

We've done it.

We've learned a great deal about how important we are to each other in the process. And how very much we need our communities.

So, for the first post-pandemic anthology Inspire Christian Writers put out, it really was a no-brainer what our them would be: Community.

We're very glad you're part of ours.

– 1 –

Blessed are the Peacemakers
Christine Hagion

Gang-bangers, thieves, drug dealers, and murderers. What could I possibly have in common with them? Nothing. And everything.

We are peacemakers. We are female. And we all have an abuse history. Beyond that, we have little in common. Yet we've become a family.

I only visit twice a year, but stay in touch with them all by letter, when I have time to write. I laugh with them, cry with them, dream with them, worry for them, pray for them—just like I do for my own grown children. Their picture sits on my mantle, where I see them every day. I wear a purple plastic wristband to remind me of their stories, and their faces. I carry them in my heart and mind throughout my days, rushing from one appointment to another.

It began with a letter from a stranger. JoAnn, an inmate, wrote me, as the founder of a nonprofit agency providing victim services, inviting me to participate in their Domestic Violence Awareness Day. She wrote: "Of the 4,000 women here in the prison, the one thing we have in common is that we are all survivors." How could I stay away?

Along the three-hour-trip to Chowchilla, I smiled, watching cattle munching on amber grass on the undulating hillside. Driving past cornfields, vineyards, and groves of almond trees, I finally saw the guard posts towering over the complex. The juxtaposition of the countryside was striking—amidst serene farmland live thousands of hardened criminals.

I turned in, appreciating the manicured lawn, outlined by large, smooth rocks, set against the backdrop of almond trees in full bloom. The landscaped driveway resembled a showcase for a new housing development. After parking, I approached security, went through the metal detectors, and sat with the other visitors while awaiting our escort. A guard accompanied us through an electronic sliding door, opening into a holding area surrounded by tall chain-link fencing, topped with circular razor wire. Our escort greeted us beyond another electronic sliding door.

Tall chain-link fencing continued around the perimeter, with signs warning: "Danger!/Peligro!" and showing a little electrocuted black stick figure. Such a stark contrast from the scenic splendor I'd enjoyed along the drive: there was no beauty at all within these grounds. Upon acres of bare ground were nondescript grey concrete buildings housing prisoners. No grass; just dirt. Not a flower or tree in sight.

Walking past a building with multiple doors attached to several small fence-enclosed areas, I wondered what they could be used for. It reminded me of the small dog runs I'd seen in an animal shelter when my daughter had picked out our puppy. In my mind's eye, I could still see cute faces of the sad, caged dogs who wanted so much to be freed, and thought how similar to the prisoners we would soon be encountering. Our escort must have noticed the curious look on my face, she explained that this building was for family visits.

This was my sixth trip to the prison in two years. I attended the second annual Domestic Violence

Awareness Day last year, and I'd been back several times to provide training to a group of prisoners, most of whom were serving life sentences. Thirty remarkable women had formed a cadre within the walls of the prison, becoming trained peer educators who would spread awareness about domestic violence within the prison — a place where I, as an abuse prevention educator — would never have access.

Inside, Katie, a peer educator, gave me a hug I could not reciprocate: my hands were full with the large box of handouts I'd brought. After showing me to my seat, she pointed to our designated table. As I set up, several of the prisoners I'd met previously came to greet me.

"So good to see you again," one said.

"When are you coming back for more training?" asked another.

We had a few moments to greet and hug one another (although it's generally frowned on in the prison, but the guards relaxed the rules slightly for the occasion). The program was starting. Five hundred women took their seats in expectation, most in blue jeans and pale blue T-shirts or white and dark-blue baseball shirts making up the prisoners' uniform.

Looking along the walls of the cafeteria, I read the hand-made posters declaring the theme for this year's event: "Stepping Up and Stepping Out."

"Peer educators, step up!" A booming voice thundered, like a drill sergeant calling troops to march in formation. Then, a stamping of numerous feet in rhythmic cadence carried a beat as two rows of eighteen peer educators, each clad in sunglasses, marched into the room, and stood along a taped line in the center of the floor. Another loud call and all the peer educators turned, about face, in unison. My father, a former Army Major, would have been proud.

"I am stepping out in memory of my mother, God rest her soul," one of the peer educators proclaimed.

"I am stepping out for the little girl who couldn't say 'no'," said another.

"I am stepping out for myself," said another, turning to face us.

"I am stepping out for my sisters." One voice after another, each one speaking with the boldness that comes from personal conviction.

"I am stepping out for my children, so that we can break the cycle."

Following the peer educator's dramatic entry, the program began. The first three speakers were among the prison staff, telling how the peer education

Christine Hagion

program had impacted their lives. The first was a female instructor of the high school completion course. While the peer educators gave a domestic violence presentation for her class, she'd read one of their handouts about the different forms of abuse (physical, verbal, sexual, financial, psychological, spiritual) — and realized, for the first time, that she was in a domestic violence relationship with her husband of 23 years. She told the audience, "I never realized it as abuse, because he never hit me." She has since divorced, and now has a healthy, nonviolent relationship with one of the officers within the institution. She was greeted with hugs and applause.

Rafael, another instructor, told a similar story, about a woman he'd lived with, along with his extremely disabled younger brother. Rafael's partner was physically abusive, and he learned from the peer educators' classroom presentation how destructive it is for children growing up witnessing domestic violence. He realized his brother was being exposed to the abuse Rafael endured. "Because of what I've learned," he said, "I will never let another person abuse me ever again."

Betty, an inmate, had escaped her batterer, who lured her back "to talk about the kids." He then attempted to murder her, strangling her with one hand and shoving a pistol into her face with the other. "But I'm alive by the grace of God," she said. "His alcoholism was my salvation. In his drunkenness, he didn't realize that he had the safety on." Betty fought back, saving herself, but was convicted for manslaughter.

Windy, one of the peer educators, shared that her parents were both addicts, and violence was an everyday occurrence. She later married a man she expected was her knight in shining armor, but he abused Windy and her baby—which died from its injuries. Incarcerated for his crime, Windy was granted parole several times, but the governor twice rescinded her release. Even behind bars, Windy considers herself free—because while she's still a prisoner, she's not being abused. She is confident of her release, someday, just like JoAnn, the prisoner who first wrote me.

I realized, while listening, that I'd been mistaken thinking there was no beauty within the grounds of the prison. The beauty was right there in front of me: inside each of the peer educators, who were doing such amazing things in this institution.

At last year's event, I'd given out five hundred purple wristbands imprinted with the words *faith*, *hope*, *courage*, and *strength*, saying that these traits would enable the prisoners to heal the wounds of abuse. Rae, one of the peer educators, was wearing her wristband. I was surprised she still had it.

"Are you kidding?," she responded. "It's my most prized possession."

Nikki, who's been released, mentioned her "sisters" in the prison. Because we are committed to the same cause — raising awareness about domestic violence — they feel like family. My educating them about abuse, and training them to do the same, developed a bond between us.

Driving home, I recognized one thing these women have within prison we're missing on the outside: the collective energy and unity to make their world better, safer. For a few hours, all racial, educational, and religious backgrounds were suspended: we were all one, stepping up and stepping out against abuse. I'm on the outside, doing the same work they are, on the inside. And each time I eat an almond or corn on the cob, I'll remember my sisters in the prison, growing a crop of peace in the California countryside.

— 2 —

Creating a Community Care Group for Connection
Deb Gruelle

[Often] only those who are experiencing a similar situation can understand. Providing appropriate avenues to express pain and grief with other believers is vital.[1]

— Debra Evans —

Sometimes, we simply need to be around people who understand. There's nothing like a pandemic hitting and shutting down the world to help us realize how

---

[1] Evans, Debra. "The Infertility Maze." *Christian Parenting Today*, Feb. 1991, p. 60.

much we need community. Reaching out to connect with others may be as easy as finding an already established group to join.

If we can't find a group, however, we may need to start one. Starting a group can feel intimidating though. When I started a community care group to help women struggling with infertility and pregnancy loss, I had no previous experience. The group was so successful, though, I led it for nearly a decade.

I learned a few things in starting this group that I want to encourage you with. I didn't need to have all the answers, I simply needed to recognize the need. Providing a space for women to meet and facilitating the group became a highlight of my difficult seventeen-year journey through infertility and pregnancy loss.

If you're hoping to start a community group to help others connect, do it! This journey of life can sometimes be arduous, and a supportive community can become a great sustainer. The results can be life-giving.

Overcoming the Fear of Starting

Part of my hesitancy to start a group stemmed from not knowing how to start, since I had never run a community group before. So, I asked a friend to help. Now we were both nervous, but we could at least bounce ideas off each other. We wondered, *what if nobody comes? What if nobody talks?*

The First Meetings

My friend and I met before the first meeting and set up a tentative agenda. We prayed. We talked about wanting to offer a safe place where women could share and be listened to, feel supported and encouraged, find hope in their relationship with God and His Word, and be brought into the presence of the Healer through prayer.

As it turned out, six women came that first night, and we had *no* problem with them being too quiet, which confirmed the need for this type of group. A few months later, my co-leader friend got pregnant again and left the group. I continued leading with occasional new co-leaders. And the women kept coming. They came every other week for the next decade.

Even though our group wasn't run perfectly, everyone was gracious as we all learned along the way. A wonderful side benefit of the deep sharing in our group was that it also created some lifelong friendships.

One of the things I found most surprising was how we found the freedom to laugh at events we had previously found traumatic. For instance, the first time my husband and I tried intrauterine insemination, I got lost while driving the vial containing the washed sperm sample from the hospital to the doctor's office for the insemination. It was only a distance of about two miles, but I didn't know the area. This was before GPS and I kept taking wrong turns. So much effort, money, and hope were riding on this. All my focus was on keeping the sperm alive and getting them to the doctor's office within the time constraints.

When I found myself on the wrong street yet again, my stomach began churning. How long would sperm live in a tube? I was told to keep them warm, so I had tucked the vial into my coat. The clock kept ticking down though with each wrong turn. My journey had become a matter of life or death. These sperm and our dream of having a baby were going to die unless I could find my way soon. By the time I finally found the doctor's office, I was near tears. If anyone had told me to relax at that point, I think I would have screamed. I was stressed!

Later though, in describing my panic to the group, we all saw the funny side of my mad rush and valiant efforts to *Save the Sperm!* Two women even shared similar stories of their sperm excursions that made us laugh until we cried. Where else could we experience comfort from others who would relate on that deep level?

Attendee Perceptions About the Group

When Virginia first came to our care group, she had just experienced her fourth miscarriage: "I was in so much pain when I arrived at the group. I wondered what I would do with six other women in pain, but then I saw the joy that you shared because you understood each other."

Sara was glad to find she wasn't alone in her struggles: "I'm so thankful for this group. Before I came, I thought I was just going crazy, but then I saw that I wasn't the only one affected so strongly by infertility."

Vicky, who'd been infertile for more than ten years and had adopted a daughter seven years earlier, expressed that being part of the group helped bring healing to her relationship with God:

> I came to this group mainly to give support, but it's really helped me too. I didn't realize that there was still a part of me that felt unloved by God because I wasn't ever able to get pregnant. But when I sit and look at all of the other women in this group, I have no trouble at all believing God loves them. I know

he does. That's helped me to realize he loves me, too.

In-Person vs. Online Care Groups

Starting an in-person community care group is a wonderful option. In-person meetings can facilitate deep sharing and healing. And there's nothing like receiving shared tears and deep, genuine hugs when you're grieving.

An online community group can be the next best thing. Online groups eliminate any geographic and travel issues (as well as world-shut-down distancing rules). An online group using Zoom or another app that allows everyone to see each other's faces and chat can be helpful. As the online leader, you may need to put some extra effort into encouraging interaction between the members.

A friend who was active in a topical Facebook group, later asked the group owner for permission to offer a weekly Zoom meeting to the women in the larger group. She advertised within the larger group and invited anyone who was interested. Her video-chat sub-group has been well-received and continues with strong attendance.

Setting Goals to Start

For my group, we started by setting some goals to define what we hoped to accomplish and later to help evaluate our progress. The goals we wanted for our group were:

- To let others know they weren't alone in their struggle.
- To provide sensitive understanding during the grief process.
- To encourage and build each other up in love.
- To provide a way to share information related to infertility, miscarriage, stillbirth, and adoption.
- To pray for each other, seek God together, and look to the Bible for answers.
- To get the word out about our group to reach the women who might benefit from it.

Whom Should We Invite?

We chose to invite women who were experiencing grief from either not being able to have a child or from losing a child. This included women experiencing infertility (both primary and secondary), miscarriage, recurrent miscarriages, stillbirth, and early infant loss.

Deb Gruelle

We chose this focus for our group because, although the struggles were different, we felt we'd still have enough in common to relate to each other.

We chose not to restrict our group to Christians but invited anyone to come who felt comfortable with meetings where we prayed for each other, shared our struggles before God, and looked for hope from the Bible. We felt this inclusivity was an opportunity to introduce God's hope to all hurting women.

Is it Time for You to Start a Community Group?

Does starting a new community group sound promising to you? If so, ask God if the longing to create a group is from Him and for this season in your life. If you choose to offer connection through a community group, may God bless your efforts, offer divine connections, provide a sense of belonging, and pass on His comfort through it.

> What a wonderful God we have…who so wonderfully comforts and strengthens us in our hardships and trials. And why does He do this? So that when others are troubled, needing our sympathy and encouragement, we can pass on to them this same help and comfort God has given us. *(2 Corinthians 1:3–4 TLB).*

— 3 —

Finding Contentment
Marilyn Siden

Not long ago I made an early run to the grocery store to pick up a few breakfast items. I've grown accustomed to wearing a mask; although I've never loved the warm, slightly moist, stifling air it produces. There is nothing quite like a mask-free cool morning breeze to get my blood moving.

David was on-duty for the morning shift that day. He always greeted everyone, wiped off carts to kill any lingering germs, stepped on the automatic door opener, and said, "Do you want a cart or a basket?"

Marilyn Siden

After that greeting, he asked, "How are you this morning?"

I gave him a rather bland, "I'm fine," answer and, without thinking, lobbed the question back at him.

With a warm smile, he responded, "I'm content."

After my brief shopping trip, I found David on my way out. I had to thank him for what he said to me and let him know I wanted to embrace those two words from now on when asked how I'm doing. He smiled broadly and responded, "Praise the Lord. I won't forget you."

I have shared my brief encounter with a number of people, and they all — one hundred percent of them — emphatically said, "I want that for my life."

It would seem this horrible, tragic, disruptive pandemic has taught most of us how to slide right past even a molecule of contentment and settle into our natural response of complaint. "I'm missing my grandchildren." "I can't even buy a decent pair of shoes." "I'm ready to eat inside a sit-down restaurant." "I want to worship at church. I miss all my church friends." No contentment here!

The complaints are as varied as the people voicing them, but "I" seems to be at the center of everything. The coronavirus has disrupted *my* way of life, and *I* don't like it. While there are momentary seconds of

Finding Contentment

gratitude, for the most part, complaining is so much easier. Everyone understands, because we have all shared the same difficulties and necessary, but uncomfortable, changes in our daily lives. It is hard to focus on the positive when so many people have died — and are still dying ... wrestled away from their loved ones. Watching and listening to the hundreds of nurses and doctors holding up cell phones and iPads for a final goodbye has broken us. We corporately appreciate their bravery for standing amidst all that isolation and death. If the truth were told, most of us are glad we are not called to do the same.

No one in my family — or for that matter, no one I know — has needed a ventilator to replace damaged lungs in order to stay alive. One nurse recently said, "The virus does not seem to care how rich you are or who you know. It hits all of us. If you could see the protective gear I need to wear just to check in on one of my patients, it would break your heart."

So David's proposition to me and perhaps to you as well is to find contentment where we least expect it. The hydrangeas in my postage stamp-size yard continue to bloom. A child down the street makes a colorful hopscotch game on the sidewalk with the challenge for anyone passing by to run its course. A mama duck with her twelve — that's right, twelve —

ducklings teaches the fine art of bobbing for anything below the surface of the water. The cloud overhead gives some momentary relief from the heat.

I wish it were as easy as deciding to be a half-full instead of a half-empty person. There are all sorts of cliché reminders: "When life serves you lemons, make lemonade." "Always look for the silver lining." "I was sad I had no shoes until I met a man who had no feet."

So what does it look like to be content in 2021 in the middle of a pandemic that has snuffed out the lives of more than three and a half million people in the world? In many parts of our planet, that microscopic deadly virus is still wreaking havoc and misery.

While all that is going on, there are other things that have swallowed up our daily lives leaving devastating destruction in their wake. How about the grandmother who recently told me she worries about her adopted grandson who is threatening suicide — at age ten? How does she find contentment? What about those who dared march in the streets with the chant about not being replaced or children living in a war-torn world, just wanting to grow up and become doctors or construction workers or raise a family? Can they find reason to be content?

The dictionary definition is an emotional state of satisfaction that can be seen as a mental state, maybe drawn from being at ease in one's situation, body, or mind. It is frequently defined as in a state of having accepted one's situation completely — the good and the downright difficult. The Apostle Paul seemed to get it. By anyone's standards, he had it rough. Shipwrecked, imprisoned, beaten, rejected — all multiple times. Yet while he was shackled in a dirty, smelly, dungeon, the guards found him singing. When he had every reason to complain and grouse about his surroundings, Paul found joy and a reason to keep going no matter his circumstances. So did David, my grocery store worker. It seems they experienced contentment not from what was going on around them but in the knowledge God is in the driver's seat.

When God is the driver in our lives, we cannot sit in our little corner of the world, claim contentment and let suffering explode at a safe distance from our comfortable surroundings. Writer Edith Kelly summed it up well when she wrote, "The further we are from the frontline, the easier it is to believe that everything is okay."

I think we really don't have a choice. As the hands and feet of Jesus, doing "something" is built into our DNA. By our very nature as Jesus followers, we can never decide that doing nothing comes anywhere near what we are called to do — not if I want that promised, but elusive contentment I crave. Perhaps — if we look to the lives of fellow followers — it sneaks up and surprises us in the process of our obedience to our calling.

Contentment came to Paul, not during all the years of his persecution of Christians, but when he decided to walk in the dust of the Rabbi. Peter found reasons to be content, even in death, when he exchanged his three denials of his Savior for a driving faith with no quit in it. He ended up laying it all on the line and beginning a movement known as "the church."

We have many models and mentors even today. They are there to remind us to be content in all we do — even wiping down carts and baskets and stepping on automatic door openers or drawing on the sidewalk to spread joy and a smile to those passing by. Those models seem to help us remember there is a certain contagious quality to living in community and, as it spreads, it just might circle the globe and end up in the most unlikely places for the benefit of the world.

– 4 –

Fitting In

Susan Sage

What a rich, personal word: community. Something many people want, and yet, a concept without an instruction manual.

My family moved every few years. We learned to blaze a path in a new place and figure out how to find our fit. Everyone wanted to know the pastor's family. We often received invitations to meals whether in a restaurant or in someone's house. Many times, we had people to our home. As my father's children, we knew we had to build meaningful relationships with everyone else's children.

The problem was not how to make new acquaintances, but how to keep them. Whenever we moved our parents told us not to hold on to these friendships because our hearts needed to have room for the people we would meet in our new home.

When we married, my husband and I lived in an area where my father had pastored. My father's name was known, as was my husband's family. It was comfortable.

Seven years later, we moved many miles from the familiar to a new area of rich green grass and variegated leaves of beauty and adventurous prospects. We were starting over. But an unfamiliar fear wrapped itself around me and dug its talons deep within.

The place of the unknown met me. No family shirttails to cling to. Not one person knew my father or all the churches he had pastored.

A strange aloneness hung on me.

I was going to have to brave the people at church without the benefit of my family name or reputation. How would I ever fit in? I couldn't go meet the pastor and introduce myself as my father's daughter.

Prayer requests. That's how I could do it. Everyone at church prays for others. If I couldn't count on a name, I would be known for my numerous health

Fitting In

issues. Every Christian wants a testimony of relying on God through physical trials, right? I could to that.

With every subsequent move from town to town and church to church, I would make it known. I suffered for the sake of Christ.

But I could also let others know I could teach. Every place we relocated, I volunteered to work with children. I'd grown up in the church and was as familiar with my Bible as most other people. I would point the little ones to Jesus. So important.

Funny thing, I was happy enough and loved to teach, but I didn't feel a sense of true belonging; I was performing as a good Christian pastor's kid should.

I still didn't know how to fit in without wearing a nameplate.

Pastor's kid. Check.

Chronic health sufferer. Check.

Teacher. Check.

Few people saw or knew the truth. I wanted to belong because of me and not the label. I couldn't ever be completely part of something if I never stepped out from behind the façade.

After another move, a friend invited me to go with her to a writing group. I'd loved to write since my early teen years, and I needed a change. She pushed and prodded several more times before I agreed to accompany her.

As my friend and I settled into a soft couch, I wanted it to swallow me. To my surprise, a woman I'd met previously greeted me as she entered. More people drifted in. Nerves screamed for me to run when introductions started. With everything in me, I wanted to tell them about my father or my health issues or that I could teach. I was convinced they needed to understand those details to get to know me. I remained planted in the couch and gave two facts: my name and how long I'd written.

As the meeting progressed, my mind swam to keep up with the conversation. These writers discussed each other's work and what might bring improvements. The leader talked about books she'd read on the craft of writing. I'd never heard of such a thing but leaned closer; I didn't miss a word.

In the next moment, the shocking happened. The facilitator turned to me and asked what I thought about what someone else had written. They wanted to know. I took a deep breath, blew it out slowly, lowered my shoulders, and gave my opinion. Ten. Twenty. Thirty seconds ticked by in silence. I fiddled with my wedding ring, then twisted at my bracelet. I crossed and uncrossed my legs, shifted my position

Fitting In

on the soft couch as the smell of diesel breezed through the open window behind me. A car door slammed in the distance. Still, I waited. Then, I watched as smiles spread across each face as if doing a wave at a football game.

I was hooked.

Week after week, I went with my friend. We shared lively discussions on the way home after each meeting. I submitted my first sample of writing. These writers I'd come to know by name and their word-crafting offered helpful comments. Excitement built every time as I took proffered suggestions home to apply them to my work.

At one of the critique group meetings, the leader mentioned a writing conference on the horizon. Once again, intrigue caught my attention. Doubt never had a chance.

Several months later, I stepped onto the holiest of grounds I've ever known. I listened with apt intent as teachers shared knowledge and wisdom. Conversations, laughter, interactions, teaching, praising God, singing, and more of each covered the next few days.

Though I didn't always understand all the communication flowing around me, and I wished a writing dictionary had accompanied the newcomer's packet, new confidence surged through me. These were my people.

Encouragement flowed between participants who were of the same mind and interests. Competition did not exist when all we wanted was to help each other stretch in the abilities God had given us. Camaraderie grew in the community of writers I'd stepped into. All too soon, the time came for our return to normal life. But would anything ever be the same?

I had found my community. I fit in.

God brought me to a place of understanding. As I walked in His purpose for me, as I continued in the gifts and strength He'd given, as I sought to live out all He had for me, He would provide the place for me to belong.

Community. Such a rich, personal word.

— 5 —

Food for Thought

D.H. Weinberg

I live in Orange County, California. Yeah, that's right. *The Real Housewives of Orange County* county. I know what you're thinking. We were thinking it, too, when we moved here. Snobby, rich people who were just into fancy cars, expensive homes, and making the scene. And yes, there are those people here, but let me tell you about my community.

We live on a dead-end street with people of all cultures, religions, and income levels. We have a lot of Persians from Iran, Mormons from Utah, and home-grown or transplanted Caucasians, Latinos, and Asians. Where once Orange County was homogeneous, it's now a box of chocolates. We love it!

Some people in our neighborhood have their own businesses, and some are retired. One neighbor works in hospice nursing, another at a car dealer, and a third at the local grocery store. Remarkably, in our community most of us don't care what job you hold, how much money you have, or how you got here. We are neighbors who help and care about each other. In fact, we're the melting pot or the salad bowl that the United States was intended to be.

What makes us a community is that we know each other. We care about each other. We're friends with each other's kids, and attend important events in each other's lives. We are also available for each other—whether it's to help in an emergency, or to borrow an egg or a teaspoon of cinnamon.

Real friendship is the essence of community. We live in an age where many people don't even know their neighbors. As suburban Americans, we are so used to going to work early, working ten hours a day, and then pulling into our garage at night. It's so easy on weekdays not to have contact with those outside our family.

So how have we built community? In a word—FOOD! In all cultures, food is the great unifier. The great barrier-breaker. If you feed them, they will come. We all know what a box of donuts does in a workplace. People come out of the woodwork, or at least out of their cubicles to kibbitz. The same is true for a neighborhood. At least it is in ours.

Food is the reason people congregate in the kitchen. Food is the reason that restaurants of every ethnicity exist. Everybody can talk about food — no Ph.D. required. Food is not just the way to a man's stomach, but the way to women and children's stomachs, too. It's the universal donor, the O blood type in society. Everybody can donate, and everybody loves a donation. Life is filled with hardship and pain, but good food almost always brings joy.

Food does more than feed us, of course. It says "I care enough about you to make this for you. I hope this will make you happy. You're important to me." These are words that are difficult to say out loud, even to our own family members at times. We're a society that's uptight about telling people how we feel — when we love them. So, food does that for us. It says "I really love you" — without the waterworks.

The people of China and Singapore understand this. One of their greetings is actually translated, "Have you eaten?" Italian grandmothers understand this. When you arrive at their house for a meal they say, "Mangia, Mangia." Most holidays and special occasions feature celebratory foods as well. It wouldn't be Christmas at our house without decorating the sugar cookies my mother always makes.

Food sharing has a domino effect. The more banana bread or key lime pie my wife makes and gives away, the more cookies, lemon bars, and dinner invitations we get in return. In fact, there are many weeks we get to eat dinner with our neighbors. We enjoy good food, their hospitality, and grow closer as we talk.

Food sharing also gives us new dinner ideas and recipes. We all get stuck in ruts answering the "What's for dinner?" question. In our family, we go to the same old favorites and standbys—hamburgers, barbeque chicken, brats with sausage and onions, and spaghetti with meat sauce.

So, how wonderful it is to get a neighbor's great eggplant parmesan recipe? How thoughtful to get the ingredients for a new casserole, soup, or salad dish? Most people love sharing a new recipe with their neighbors, and most people enjoy receiving one.

In our area, we have a lot of Chinese, Thai, Italian, Indian, and Middle Eastern restaurants. Sometimes we go out to eat with our neighbors. Community is also built sharing chicken tikka, lamb gyros, fish tacos, baked lasagna, or pad Thai. Eating with good friends, whether the food is home-cooked or restaurant-bought, usually brings laughter, jokes, stories, news of local happenings, and fun to any gathering.

What does the Bible say about breaking bread with others? Sharing food and drink is all over the New Testament. Jesus's first miracle is turning water into wine at a Cana community wedding. Several times, Jesus also multiplies bread and fish to feed people in a community who have gathered to hear Him speak. Most importantly, at the Last Supper, Jesus uses food and wine to illustrate His body and blood — shed for all of us. He commands His disciples to practice communion with the bread and the wine, together and in remembrance of Him.

In fact, sharing food was one of the hallmarks of the early Church, and attracted so many believers. *They devoted themselves to the apostles' teaching and to the fellowship, to the breaking of bread and to prayer.* (Acts 2:42 NIV) Can you imagine what would happen today if most churches were as dedicated to meeting and sharing food with their community as they were in the days of the early Church?

Jesus also commands us to share food and what we have with the poor in our community. For I was hungry and you gave me something to eat, I was thirsty and you gave me something to drink, I was a stranger and you invited me in. (Matthew 25:35 NIV) Jesus realizes we all have physical needs in addition to spiritual needs. He says, Love your neighbor as yourself. (Matthew 22:39 NIV) Community is built when, as Christians, we care about everybody in our community.

In my neighborhood, we do other things that bring us a sense of community. We attend Neighborhood Watch meetings. We go homeowner's meetings. We have July 4th picnics and fireworks in the street. We have block parties. We also walk our dogs every morning around the neighborhood and catch up. Many of us go to a local church, mosque, or synagogue as well.

However, *food*, more than anything, has melded my neighborhood into a vibrant community. Food allows us to ask a husband how his wife is doing with her illness–when we bring over the homemade bread she loves. It provides a reason to visit someone's home and comfort them after a loss, when just showing up empty-handed might be awkward. It says, "I remembered your kid's birthday" and "Congratulations on your anniversary today."

It may seem simplistic, but sharing food may be one of the easiest ways to build community. If there was more sharing of food in the world, there would probably be more joy, fewer social barriers, and many stronger and more vibrant communities. Plus, as in the early Church, many neighbors might discover God, the Creator of all food, and His goodness, love, and grace.

— 6 —

A Heart for Community
Christy Hoss

Blue and red lights flashed as I watched the ambulance take Kevin, my husband of fifteen years, away in a whirlwind off to a hospital in San Francisco, sixty miles from our home in Santa Rosa.

A few hours earlier we had been celebrating Mother's Day with his mom at our home. Kevin gripped his chest, his face ashen with beads of sweat on his forehead. As a CPR instructor, I knew what was happening. Kevin was having a heart attack.

Kevin was born with a congenital heart defect. One of his valves did not work. He'd been monitored by doctors since childhood and was not expected to live past thirty. Now my forty-year-old husband was on his way to our health care provider's heart specialty center, facing open heart surgery.

I'd held in my emotions the entire time in the private emergency room with Kevin. I needed to stay strong for him. We'd prayed for God to give us strength. But watching the ambulance drive off Sunday evening, my entire body went numb, and my brain clouded. What just happened? Was this real or a nightmare? Desperate, I called my only sister, Cindy.

"They ... took ... Kevin ... away." My stilted words brought immediate questions I could not answer. Hearing her voice broke the dam of my "be brave and stay strong" front and I convulsed with uncontrollable sobs. In-between gasping for air and nose blows, I managed to relay the past three hour's traumatic events. Cindy would fly up on Friday to help out.

After collecting myself, I worried my way home, driving the type of drive where you're suddenly at your destination and you can't remember how you got there, like you're in a dark tunnel with no lights.

Thankfully, Kevin's parents had stayed with the kids, and they were ready for bed when I arrived. Andrew, then twelve, and Jacob, nine, went to sleep after their prayers. My daughter GraceAnne, seven,

A Heart for Community

insisted upon sleeping with me. Not knowing what was happening frightened her. It frightened me, too.

Before going to bed I called my friend Tammy. My cloudy, overwhelmed mind needed direction and she gave it to me. Tammy and her daughter would stay at our home and take care of the kids.

I had no clue how long I'd be gone. Dumping your parenting responsibilities on another person, trusting them with the lives of your offspring with no idea of when you would return is the worst thing a mom could do. My heart had already been ripped out of my chest when they took Kevin away.

Before I drove to San Francisco, Tammy met to pray with me. Praying was something I hadn't done in almost a year. Disenchanted by a Christian organization, I had turned my back on God. Unable to sleep on Sunday night, I called the 800 number for K-LOVE radio to speak to a pastor. After praying with me, I hung up and fell to my knees, begging for God's forgiveness. His Spirit flooded me from my head to my toes, redeeming me once again. Getting up, I turned on the radio. A song that had been tugging at my heartstrings since I walked away from God played instantly. Its lyrics confirmed God's love for me.

Walking through the sliding doors of the hospital entrance, a giant red heart sculpture greeted me. It would become my anchor in the coming storm. That night I slept in a chair next to Kevin, holding his hand and praying all night long.

First thing Wednesday morning the nurses came for Kevin. With his parents and me at his side, we prayed together before they wheeled him into surgery. The doctor explained the entire procedure, but, in my half-worried half-trusting God state of mind, I couldn't keep the details straight. We were to wait the three hours in a small room filled with other people waiting for the phone to ring and the attendant to call your name with an update. Three hours might as well have been a lifetime. I spent them praying and listening to encouraging music. I wandered into the tiny chapel for some quiet meditation where I begged God not to take my husband from me. While pacing the hallway, my phone rang. It was K-LOVE asking, "How can we pray for you today?"

Are you kidding me?

At the very moment I needed prayer, my radio station reached out to me.

Back in the waiting room, the phone rang.

"Christy Hoss?" The attendant answering the phone called my name.

A Heart for Community

I flew from my chair to take the phone. Kevin was in the recovery room. I would be allowed a short visit with my sleeping husband.

Tubes were hanging out of him everywhere like a Frankenstein experiment. I whispered "I love you" as I stroked his ear. His blood pressure spiked, and the nurse asked, "What did you do?" I have always loved his ears. It was a gesture of my love and he had felt it.

Kevin's mom stayed that night with me in the city. Settled into our hotel, the hospital called to say he'd be taken off the ventilator and was breathing on his own.

"Mom. I'm going to take a shower and have a cry. Please just let me be. Just let me cry." The shower walls supported my trembling body as I wailed like a professional mourner. It was a long, hard cry, the kind that relieves the stress held in from the past three days.

Every time I entered the hospital, I saluted the big red heart, my symbol of hope.

With Kevin awake and doing well, the doctor said he would most likely be going home on Monday. One tiny lightbulb turned on in my dark tunnel. There would be good news to share with my visiting sister who sponsored a hotel room for the kids and me to enjoy a hot tub and pool that weekend. A welcome relief from our troubles.

Monday morning, I saluted the big heart once more expecting to take Kevin home. Instead, I found him attached to an AED device, transferring back to intensive care. His heart had stopped several times. The light bulb in my tunnel burned out.

Two weeks of daily saluting the big red heart passed. I shuffled the kids between grandparents and friends. Bills started rolling in and I had no idea how we would make ends meet. I was certain we would lose everything. How could I put food on the table or pay the mortgage without any income?

It was going on the fourth week of Kevin's hospitalization. Sunday morning as I'm driving to visit Kevin, my phone rings. It's the hospital. Kevin is being discharged. My foot presses hard on the accelerator and I pray there are no speed traps.

I have to tell someone the good news. I call Tammy. She's at church and the pastor is just about to pray for Kevin. I hear Tammy yell above the pastor, "He's coming home!" and a "Praise God" collective roar from the congregation lifts my spirits. I salute the big red heart one last time and bring my husband home.

Kevin was out of work and on disability for four months back in 2007. We had very little income and

A Heart for Community

no savings to cover our costs. Fortunately, we had good insurance so medical bills were not an issue. But what about groceries, utilities, and the $2,000 mortgage?

Community surrounded us like a constant hug.

Visiting the classroom where I worked, the students bunched around me in a group hug and gave me homemade cards. The school secretary made sure I got paid for the entire month of May, even though I hadn't worked one day.

Community means having a big heart ready to serve the needs of others.

Every other day after Kevin came home, the church's meal ministry brought a dinner for three months. Each one was more than enough to enjoy many leftovers. Tuesday dinner was always pizza for us. Every week after Kevin's surgery as I picked up our order, the manager smiled and said, "No charge." My friends from another pizza place pooled their tips and gave us $200. Cards poured in with get-well wishes, checks and cash. When it came time to pay the mortgage, an anonymous donation in the exact amount I needed came in the mail.

From that awful night in the emergency room to the day Kevin returned to work, God saw it fit to involve people from every community to help us — from our church family, to a K-LOVE prayer line calling at the right time, to family and friends, and anonymous people all willing to help us in our time of need.

Community cares for one another.

I realize now why I saluted the big red heart in the hospital entry. It represents community because every one of our needs were met by big hearts.

— 7 —

Indemic

Terrie Hellard-Brown

Pandemic
Stay inside
    For protection
Distance
    For prevention
Wear masks
    For preservation
Outwardly
    During a pandemic
        They may be blessings

Terrie Hellard-Brown

Inwardly
    They become endemic
        As we accept the "new normal"
            Live in fear
                And stop connecting
Some experience an "indemic"
The cure:
Tearing down the walls
    Getting real
        Becoming vulnerable
           And transparent
It's a risk
Drawing closer to one another
    Embracing
        Communicating
           Hearing
                Being heard
It's a risk
Giving up the masks
    That the real person
        Warts and all
           Can be seen
                And known
It's a risk
But it's a risk worth taking

Indemic

In the pandemic
We learned that living behind closed doors
        And distanced from one another for too long
            Is painful
Some have lived that way for years
        In self-quarantined "indemics"
Staying locked away may be safe
        But it's empty
             Lonely
                  Is it really living at all?
Risk
        For community
Live
        For connection
Love
        For communion
It's the gift of being human
        It's the joy of being truly alive

— 8 —

Intentional Isolation

Randy Brundage

In the early morning, while it was still dark, Jesus got up, left the house, and went away to a secluded place, and was praying there. Mark 1:35 NASB

It's Valentine's Day, 2020. I'm sixty years old. I've been living alone for the first time in my life for a year now.

I'm at a Christian singles dance. At past dances, I'd danced with many women, some I already knew, and some I'd just met. I was often out on the floor, dancing recklessly, without care, and without pause. But tonight, I'm mostly sitting alone on a chair in the corner and away from the dance floor.

I'm approached by Rita[2]. She's about my age, a widow, a little shorter than me, with dark hair, glasses, a pretty face, and a very nice figure. I don't know her well, but I know her well enough to know that she's a very kind lady with a genuine Christian faith. Rita talks to me and describes another lady who she says is a friend of a friend who she's supposed to save a place for. *Why is she telling me this?*

We talk a little about writing, as she's a published author. As she walks away, I'm pretty sure she wants me to ask her to dance, but I don't. I leave the dance early.

When the COVID Pandemic of 2020 arrives, I take advantage of the opportunity to continue my isolation.

***

Jesus isolated himself on many occasions. Mark 1:35-39 is a good example. He had just gone through an intense couple of days healing people and casting out demons. Then, early in the morning while it was still dark, He went to a secluded place to pray. Some

---

[2] The names *Rita*, *Dorothy*, and *Tiffany* in this piece are not the real names of the people concerned.

of His disciples interrupted His down time and said, "Everyone's looking for you!"

Jesus's response was, "Okay, let's get out there. It's time to get back to work and preach the Word. After all, that's why I'm here."

In Mark 6:45-52, after feeding five thousand followers, Jesus sent His disciples in a boat to cross the Sea of Galilee and then He went to a mountain to pray. Soon afterwards, He walked on water and rescued His disciples from a storm.

In the Garden of Gethsemane, Mark 14:32-42, He took time to pray to His Father in Heaven, for He knew bad things were about to happen. After praying, He returned to His disciples and faced the soldiers who arrested Him, which led to His death on the cross.

In every case, after brief isolation, Jesus returned to the community to act.

***

It's Valentine's Day, 2021. I'm not feeling lonely this year, but rather relieved that I don't have the burden of taking care of anyone but myself. I watch via Facebook Live the *Intentional Relationships for Singles* book launch. I know Dan Houk, a local pastor, who is one of the co-authors. There's a lot of interaction between the authors and the online participants. It feels good to be, on some level, connected with other singles. It's interesting that the book launch happens to be on Valentine's Day, which is often an awkward day for the unmarried and unattached.

A few weeks later, Dan asks me to lead a small group for a twelve-week Zoom study of the book. I reluctantly agree to serve. In my season of saying no, I'm saying yes. It's my first step toward getting out of isolation and into the community.

***

It's July ninth, 2021. I'm at an annual singles retreat. Down some steep hills through pine trees, I can see Lake Tahoe glistening. As always, I'm blown away by the lake's astounding beauty.

As I walk into a room containing over two hundred fellow singles, my first inclination is to hide in the back row like I'd done at the previous retreat. Instead, I intentionally decide to sit near the front. For this year's retreat, Dan Houk is one of the featured speakers and I'm a small group leader.

***

It's Thursday, July fifteenth, 2021. I'm at a potluck in honor of Kris Swiatocho, an icon in the singles world and coauthor of *Intentional Relationships for Singles*. There are about ten of us, all unmarried. I'm the only man.

Intentional Isolation

One of the advantages of having a girlfriend or wife is having someone to handle my part of a potluck. Another advantage is getting to use the carpool lane. I don't have a girlfriend or wife, so I bring three boxes of carefully selected store-bought cheese snacks and a big bowl from home.

Dorothy, who's about my age, says, "Now Randy, you know, there is other food you can buy that would be more suitable for a potluck."

Tiffany, a woman in her thirties, tells me she thinks the bowl I brought is too large — more appropriate for popcorn or chips or something, but not for cheese snacks.

Kris, who's a bubbly blond about my age, joins the dispute as a peacemaker.

When Kris autographs my copy of the book, she wrote her signature and the words "See Isaiah 6:8." For me, this verse says, "Randy, it's time to step up."

If only I'd been more intentional earlier in my isolation.

Then I heard the voice of the Lord, saying, "Whom shall I send, and who will go for Us?" Then I said, "Here am I. Send me!" (Isaiah 6:8 NASB)

– 9 –

Knowing They Are There

Malcolm Mackinnon

Excitedly, I sat down as the game started. England's big moment had arrived, a quarter-final match against Ukraine in the European Championships. Such opportunities didn't come along very often.

But as I looked along the sofa, nobody was there. Where were my buddies? Where were my fellow supporters? Where were my old England-watching friends? I knew where they were: still in England! But this wasn't their fault. After all, I was the one who had moved to Santa Clara, California. And nobody had made me come on holiday to Maui, especially during the soccer finals. So here I sat, alone, at 9 a.m., drinking tea, as the drama unfolded. I thought about my friends in England, where it was 8 p.m., eating and drinking together, enjoying the game and each other's company.

But one thing encouraged me. Even if I couldn't see them, I felt their presence; not physically next to me, admittedly, but certainly in spirit. The frequent texts and WhatsApp messages, along with many humorous photos, kept reminding me that my soccer community hadn't abandoned me. Whatever the outcome of the match, whether we had collectively won or lost, we would still rejoice or mourn together, even across 6,000 miles.

It strikes me the Christian community is not that different.

Every Christian has come to Christ on their own, leaving their old environments of sin and being prepared to forsake anything and everything that belonged to their old life. The Christian is rightly labeled an alien and stranger in this world following their conversion. And, often, as we look along our spiritual sofa, we find no one physically sitting next to us.

We may now feel like strangers in our secular place of work, we may be treated as aliens in our school, regarded as foreigners in our neighborhood, or even in our home, all because of the faith we profess. The loneliness and sense of isolation can often be more than we think we can bear. However, it's worth remembering how the Bible encourages us.

Even when we feel alone, we are not alone. There exists a cloud of witnesses, both dead and alive, rejoicing with us, supporting us, praying for us, sympathizing with our struggles, and empathizing with our personal times of apparent loneliness. Although we don't see them, we remind ourselves regularly that we serve a God who brings us not just into a relationship with Him, but also with each other.

We belong to a collective community of outsiders, all different, drawn from every background, period, and country, who first approached God alone, but who then realized the vastness of the kingdom community into which He had placed them.

The writer to the Hebrews reminds us that the heroes of faith, *did not receive the things promised; they only saw them and welcome them from a distance, admitting that they were foreigners and strangers on earth* (Heb.11:13 NIV). He reminds us that such people, *are looking for a country of their own* (Heb.11:14 NIV). Later, in that same 11th chapter, the author continues by saying, despite being commended for their faith, *none of them received what had been promised, since God had planned something better for us so that only together with us would they be made perfect* (Heb.11:39-40 NIV).

They knew times of loneliness, they endured moments where it seemed no fellow believers existed, where nobody shared their faith, nor was prepared to take the same kind of risk. But they persevered, reminding themselves of how many had gone through the same experiences before them, and how many would follow later. They knew one day they would meet every like-minded Christian, gathered before God's glorious assembly, and rejoice eternally with their true kindred spirits.

As we anxiously look along our sofa in times of trial, even if it seems unoccupied, it is crucial to remember that not only is our room already filled with our spiritual team-mates, cheering us on, but God is sitting right next to us. Knowing they are there is what helps us endure.

– 10 –

Lost in the Crowd
Debbie Jones Warren

As a little girl, I lived with my parents on a large mission station in southern Nigeria. Both my mom and dad taught at a high school on the outskirts of Egbe, a rural town surrounded by savannah brush and tropical rainforest.

The other families on the compound became our close friends and seemed more like relatives than neighbors because of our daily interactions. In keeping with this family feeling, we called each adult Aunt or Uncle. Their children essentially took the place of my cousins who lived across the ocean in the U.S.

Every few weeks, all the families on the compound gathered in a backyard to share a potluck meal. I loved those relaxing family gatherings. After dinner, we played games, performed skits, and sang cheerful hymns.

During summer mornings, we did our chores, then rode bikes around the compound. I'd play with Matchbox® cars with my brothers and their friends in the soft dirt of our front yard. In the afternoons, we hiked up a narrow path through the underbrush behind our neighbors' homes to the swimming pool constructed along a granite slab. The cool water refreshed us under the hot, equatorial sun.

On Sundays, we worshipped together at the Nigerian church in town. After lunch and a rest hour, five girls my age came to our living room where Mom taught a Bible story, then served hot tea with milk and sugar.

Two weeks after I turned six, I boarded one of the planes in our mission's fleet of single-engine aircraft and, with the other kids from our station, flew four hundred miles north to Kent Academy. In the village of Miango, our mission organization operated a boarding school for grades one through nine, that adhered to the American educational system.

Lost in the Crowd

When I entered the crowded dining room that first evening, the clinking of plates and utensils filled me with an overwhelming sense of homesickness. The unfamiliar chatter and laughter were so far removed from my beloved family at home. I felt lost in the crowd of strangers.

At the end of that lonely semester, I was thrilled to return to my Egbe home. We had a Christmas potluck at my friend Betsie's house. Strings of white fairy lights hung from the branches of tall trees on either side of her backyard, creating a bubble of brightness in the dark, African night. I was in paradise.

Walking up to a long table on the grass off the back porch, my mom placed two rectangular baking pans covered with tin foil. I peeked under one lid. "Yay! You made macaroni and cheese because it's my favorite. We didn't get that in the dorm."

Lifting the foil on the smaller pan, I took a deep whiff. "And chocolate fudge, too! I haven't had fudge in *forever*." I stepped close and looked up at Mom. "At school, I missed you and your yummy food."

Mom hugged me. "I missed you too, Sweetie." Tears glistened in her eyes.

After we ate and set our plates aside, the happy group sang hymns. We had no songbooks, but the grown-ups belted out the hymns from memory —

every single verse. Sitting on the ground in front of my parents, I hugged my knees and swayed back and forth as the beautiful voices flowed over me. I was home. Home with people who knew who I was and how I fit in to this small community of family and friends.

Four blissful weeks flew by, and in January my brothers and I flew to Kent Academy again. Only the thought of my parents' two-week visit to us in April kept me going during the lonely months.

From then on, I lived at home only during summers and Christmas vacations through eleventh grade. The only exception was for fifth grade when we flew to California for furlough.

Through the years in the artificially intimate surroundings of dorm life, my classmates eventually became as close as sisters and brothers. However, I often felt alone during the busy activities of school life, longing for my family and other close relationships of my Egbe family back home.

My senior year of high school coincided with a furlough, so we moved back to California. It was wonderful to be with my parents and siblings every day. But just a week after my high school graduation, I hugged Mom and Dad goodbye at San Francisco airport, and they returned to their ministry in Nigeria.

On my own for college and free from the mission's strict rules, I rebelled against my parents' expectations. However, I desperately sought to replace the community I had lost in my upheaval from Nigeria to California. Attempting to fit in with my peers, I followed the partying crowd. Yet, that lifestyle left me empty and discouraged. How could I replace my childhood sisters and brothers? And how on earth could I marry a man I hadn't known all my life?

God provided a girlfriend who liked to party but had also been raised in the church. On Sundays, we'd attend services with her family, and the friendly atmosphere reminded me of the camaraderie I'd experienced in my Nigerian community. The familiar Bible readings, favorite hymns, and families sitting together in pews brought solace to my searching soul.

A youth Bible study on Friday nights soon took the place of parties. I discovered the best of both worlds. Those kids had a heart for following God yet still had loads of fun. I no longer needed to follow rules for rules' sake but out of love for God who invited me into His family as His adopted daughter.

In my last year of college, I started dating a handsome young man, Chris Warren, whom I met in fifth grade at the church my family attended during our

Debbie Jones Warren

furlough. After two years of dating and engagement, we married and began our own family.

Soon we had three kids. When the oldest began kindergarten, we entered him in a public school up the street. It was a dream come true walking my son to classes, pushing our youngest one in the stroller, and meeting up with friends. Being together as a family each evening began to make up for the years I had spent apart from mine at boarding school.

A neighbor invited us to attend the church around the corner. There, I met more moms whose kids attended the same school. Walking between church, school, and home with my kids brought me joy, and I began to recapture the sense of community I had cherished on our mission station as a child. With budding friendships for my kids and me, I was beginning to feel seen and known. Like I belonged.

A few months later, I went with the church women on a weekend retreat. At dinner time, I strolled alone down the hill from my cabin at the retreat center. Nearing the dining room, I heard the clinking of plates and utensils, the chatter and laughter of a happy crowd, and my stomach constricted with familiar waves of homesickness. *Will I feel lost in the crowd again?*

Stepping through the doorway, I scanned the boisterous group and my stomach tightened. Slowly and deliberately, I placed one foot in front of the other and sauntered up the aisle between rows of tables. My heart pounded like a drum.

Then I spied one of my cabinmates several tables away. Her eyes crinkled as she smiled, and she waved a hand above her head. "Over here, Debbie. We've saved you a seat."

That night as I lay in bed, my tummy filled with a good meal and my heart with an uplifting Bible message, I realized I'd again found my community. A fellowship of compassionate women, forging friendships, nurturing families, and studying God's Word.

And the food was much better than dorm food.

> God decided in advance to adopt us into his
> own family by bringing us to himself through
> Jesus Christ. This is what he wanted to do,
> and it gave him great pleasure.
> (Ephesians 1:5 NLT)

– 11 –

Lydia

Debra Celovsky

She sat on a large, flat stone wrapped in her light cloak against the slight chill of early morning. The breeze, too, was slight, whispering down the folds of the massive escarpment to the north, and riffling the nearby stream. The waters of the Gangites were dappled in soft light that eased through overhanging branches of bay trees and willowy bushes lining its banks. It was quiet. The newborn Sabbath was not quite ready to stretch and yawn and utter its first sounds of the day.

Debra Celovsky

Each week Lydia anticipated this time by herself before the group arrived. Settled on her favorite rock in a grassy clearing, she would take a deep breath, close her eyes, and prepare her mind for prayer. Her busy life of family and business would be set aside for a while. She would sit still, quieting her mind.

This morning, however, she had trouble concentrating. She felt odd, as though she was standing in front of a door that was about to swing open revealing … she knew not what.

Her mind drifted to the place of her birth, Thyatira, that loud, boisterous city of commerce just across the Aegean and many miles inland. She was, in fact, known by the name of that region. Her husband used to say, with a mischievous twinkle, "Well, it is better than being called Thyatira." Remembering him was always bittersweet. His untimely death years before had left her with young children and a growing business. Family members had helped with the children as she struggled to come to grips with this shattering new reality. But, her business skills had served her endeavors well. In fact, very well. Hard years, but productive. She marveled, even now, at her success.

Her vocation was both honorable and profitable. Dyed fabrics of reds and purples were especially sought after, and she, with her warm personality and

Lydia

high standards, had found skilled laborers. She was proud of the products she sold.

Yet, there were always questions in her mind about — what? Meaning? Purpose?

The breeze was faint now, and light was growing. She saw ripples in the water where fish were rising for morning insects. A tentative birdcall was answered by another. The strange sense of unease prompted her to stand, hugging her cloak about her. Then she sat down again. Suddenly she prayed out loud:

"What, O God, would you say to me today?"

She waited, but the memories accelerated. Thyatira held a stew of religions, including Jewish merchants she had met in the course of her business and their fascinating religious practices. As a citizen of Rome, she was familiar with the Roman pantheon of gods, but found this utter devotion to one God compelling.

Then, she met women who went to synagogue, and friendships developed. "Come and worship with us," they had urged her. So, she did. It was very strange … the reading of Scripture, the voice of the rabbi, and prayer to Jehovah.

Lydia loved worshipping with these women with their devotion and ease of companionship. She remembered thinking: *There is something here. And it is not by chance.*

She closed her eyes again and prayed: *In all of these things I do recognize your hand, O God.*

"Come to our house with your family for Shabbat dinner," a friend had said one day. They did, and were warmly welcomed by the friend's many relatives. "We will explain everything," said an elderly woman, taking her hand and leading her to the carefully arranged table. Lydia was moved as the meal progressed and the symbolism of each course was explained. It was rich in meaning, and meaning was what she yearned for. In fact, she seemed to live in a constant state of yearning.

The idea of a messiah was intriguing. "I don't quite know what to think about that," she had said with a small frown while sitting with her parents one evening. Did it mean eventual insurrection? And who? When? How? And what about the supposed messiah who the Romans had executed years ago? Rumors continued to spread about increasing numbers of His followers. *Why be devoted to a dead messiah?*

As her business grew, she decided to move her family from Asia to Macedonia. Philippi was attractive as a fairly wealthy city where there would be tax advantages. Living just inland from the port city of Neapolis, her new venture would be conveniently located for importing fabrics produced in Thyatira.

Parting from her friends and her synagogue had been difficult. "Although there is no synagogue in Philippi, you will certainly find devout women there as well," they reassured her.

She had purchased a large house, moved her children and parents across the straits, and settled in. The years in Philippi were happy, prosperous ones. Her friends in Thyatira had been right. With its small Jewish population, and a quorum of ten devout men not to be found, there was no synagogue in Philippi. But, early on, she had met a few women who met by the Gangites stream to pray, and she had joined them. As time went on, she was the one leading them in prayer.

I thank you, O God, for the friendships you've provided here over the years. They are precious to me. I thank you for the many hours of prayer we have shared in this place.

Lydia had, over those years, memorized a number of psalms. Increasingly, there were stirrings in her heart … a deep, welling desire to know the true, the living God. This morning, she prayed the fifth Psalm:

Give ear to my words, O Lord,
consider my meditation.
For to You I will pray.
My voice You shall hear in the morning, O Lord;
In the morning I will direct it to You,
and will look up.

Words from the twenty seventh Psalm, too, rose in her mind:

> *When You said, 'Seek My face,'*
> *my heart said to You, 'Your face, Lord,*
> *I will seek.'*

She heard laughter as women walked down the gentle slope toward the stream. Lydia smiled. Some were Greek, women as intrigued by the concept of Jehovah God as she had been those years ago. They were touched, too, by the fervent prayer offered in this quiet place. Recently, one of the younger women had said, "There is a kind of presence here. Maybe," she had lowered her eyes, "the God."

On this morning, as they approached, Lydia felt a stirring, like a breath of expectation being drawn deep inside. *What is it? What is it?*

It is like, the answer seemed to come unbidden, and she hardly dared think such a thing, *it is like the breath of God, Lydia, the true, the living God.*

The group appeared, walking through the trees, greeting her with smiles, and settling on other large rocks scattered around the bank of the stream. There was always a kind of Sabbath joy in the way the women arrived, and she loved them for it. After a few moments they quieted and she began gathering her thoughts to speak to them before they began to pray.

Lydia

Suddenly, footsteps could be heard hurrying down the path, the sound of pebbles scattering. The steps slowed as someone moved through the trees. Then, a man burst into the clearing. He was not tall, but radiated a great energy. With lively eyes he surveyed the group of astonished women. Then, his face broke into a huge grin and he exclaimed, "Hello, there! My name is Paul! I have found you! God be praised!"

Stunned, Lydia stared at him in wonder. Her heart seemed to expand, and her spirit to respond to some powerful, mysterious call.

In years to come, her memory would infuse that miraculous moment with a holy radiance. For on that glorious day, the gospel of Jesus Christ entered Europe through her community of praying women.

– 12 –

The Murmuration of Community

Tessa Burns

A collection of thousands of small dark birds darts through a dusky blue sky weaving in and out of each other. I am in awe that they don't collide. Not one falls to the ground. The dance continues for several minutes to the subtle song the beat their iridescent wings create. I hear the hum of myriad feathers stirring the air, igniting vibrations through the overhanging twilight. Like waves of the sea, they swirl in a cyclone, rise to their invisible mountain peak only to descend like a sudden drop on a roller coaster. This mysterious ballet floats across the sky until the innate current drifts out of sight. I stare at the silent firmament, slowly recovering from the hypnotic atmosphere. The murmuration of Heaven.

Creation repeats its song in experiences like this. The idea that thousands of birds could fly in circles and waves across the sky displaying such intuitive responses to each other in the dance of murmuration is astounding. No bird takes the lead. Each soars in its own current in what may look at times to be chaos as it flies in and out and around the others. The individual paint splash of movement across the airy canvas is instinctively choreographed in a unifying dance. Might this display reflect the tapestry of the body of Christ? A community diverse in unique presentation, gifting, and expression, yet, when each part comes together a mesmerizing work of art appears. A masterpiece created by the hand of God.

Each of us who has received the gift of redemption is set on the course to participate in this murmuration.

1 Corinthians 12:12 (ESV) says, "For just as the body is one and has many members, and all the members of the body, though many, are one body, so it is with Christ."

The Murmuration of Community

Like a flock of birds dances and dodges together in murmuration, each following its own flight path, so moves the body of Christ. "In Him we live and move and have our being" (Acts 17:28 ESV). We each travel our distinctive path, displaying our own gifting, and expression. We move in and around each other as we traverse this earth to proclaim the redeeming power of our Savior. Some may use their voice, hands, or feet. Others, their eyes or ears. Yet all move to the beat of one heart. The heart of God.

Jeremiah 31:33 (ESV) says, "'For this is the covenant that I will make with the house of Israel after those days,' declares the Lord: 'I will put my law within them, and I will write it on their hearts. And I will be their God, and they shall be my people.'"

I cannot tell you what God has called you to outside of what is clearly written in His Word. Jesus gets right to the priority in Matthew 22:37-39: love God, love your neighbor. Outside of these commands, I don't know how God might ask you to demonstrate the gift He has made you to the world. I may see your talent or personal bent and assume how you might be utilized to bring the good news to your circle of influence. But only God truly knows every detail. It is up to each of us to find our specific path by leaning into the leading of the Holy Spirit.

John 14:26 (ESV) says, "But the Helper, the Holy Spirit, whom the Father will send in my name, he will teach you all things and bring to your remembrance all that I have said to you."

When we follow the current or our flight path, pursuing the heart of God for ourselves, we intuitively move together in variant unison. Like our amazing bodies, as each part performs its role, the whole work symbiotically together. The hand doesn't remind the heart to beat, or the eyes to see or the brain to think. By His Word, God set the order into place. He breathed humankind into existence and miraculously the design of life was set in motion. A living breathing creature, who could walk, run, dance. So began the human traverse on this planet.

God made community: Adam and Eve and the multiplicity thereafter. And here we are, eons of history behind us, continuing the dance of creation. We weave in and out and around each other. We pirouette to the song of our King. At times we fly alongside another or move to the front of the v-formation to let others rest. When our strength wanes we can recuperate with the support of the lift from the group's current. We drop the color given us on the canvas for a certain time, or specific season. As each of us diligently offers our part, an incredible

The Murmuration of Community

tapestry is revealed. A fluid river of color washes across the pages of our generation.

The collective behavior is repeated across species. Fish swim in schools. Their orchestrated flow causes them to swim in a shimmering, twisting swarm to thwart predators in the deep blue. A bee's backend wiggle helps direct others in the hive to find food or protect the queen. When a queen is placed, individual bees will converse down a line creating a literal bee march to establish the hive around the queen. The Bible speaks of locusts in Proverbs 30. They have no leader, yet all march in rank. They know their part and are diligent to perform it. The behavior not only benefits the individual but the group.

These creatures respond intuitively. They do not become exact replicas. Instead, each learns their role, not expecting others to be just like them. Individuals add to the community their unique understanding and experience. The differences add to the intelligence of the collective. This diversity brings richer knowledge and depth to the whole. We do not all have the same experiences. We do not all have the same expression. We may not look alike, sound alike, or even like the same things, but we, the body of Christ, are one. We are all needed to bring the fullness of life to this world.

The truth is, not everyone is going to want to listen to what I have to say, or how I might say it. But that person may listen to you, or see your art, or writing, or kindness, and take notice and stop to turn their eyes in the direction of your source. How you share the good news of the gospel may not look like how I do, or how another does. In fact, it is better if it doesn't. We are all made in the image of God. He has breathed His life into each one of us. We all have access to the Helper, the Holy Spirit, to place our footsteps where He leads.

You might wear hiking boots, I might wear sneakers, another may sport oxfords or stilettos. How and where our feet trod will be different. Joshua 1:3 (ESV) says, "Every place that the sole of your foot will tread upon I have given to you." Where are your feet? With the help of the Holy Spirit, we will fulfill our collective goal by being our individual selves. We may dart through the sky weaving in and out and around each other. I pray we don't collide or cause another to fall to the ground, but instead focus on our place in the dance.

May each of us play our instrument well, guided by the great conductor. A symphonic masterpiece beautiful in expression.

The Murmuration of Community

How beautiful upon the mountains are the feet of him who brings good news, who publishes peace, who brings good news of happiness, who publishes salvation, who says to Zion, 'Your God reigns.' (Isaiah 52:7 ESV)

– 13 –

My People

Robynne Elizabeth Miller

After maneuvering into a shaded roadside parking space, I turned off the ignition and closed my eyes. As soon as I'd first entered the conference grounds, intending to drive around the loop several times to get my bearings, I'd rolled down all the windows, anxious to drink in the heady blend of redwoods, rhododendrons, and hope.

Four-and-a-half hours' worth of driving, thinking, praying, and worrying hadn't changed my disposition in the least. I was overwhelmed. Scared. And, yet, where I knew I was supposed to be. I took a deep, deep breath and opened my eyes.

Few cars lined the main road which cut through the heart of the forested campus, so I had found a spot directly across from the main administration building and almost in front of an historic-looking chapel. Above the road, a gracefully arched footbridge connected the chapel side with the other. Two young men chatted as they crossed it, dappled in flecks of soft sunlight trickling through the thick canopy. They looked calm, relaxed, *confident*.

For a brief moment, I envied them. Although about twice their age, I was anything but calm, relaxed, and confident. More like anxious, nervous, and full of self-doubt. Although I had always wanted to be a writer, my first career had headed into business, and then my beautiful, complicated brood of adopted and biological children had filled my days and weeks and years.

As soon as my mind flitted toward my family, guilt overtook my envy.

My kids—my beautiful, exuberant, chaotic little brood … and the loving, supportive, kind husband I'd left behind in our corner of the Sierra Nevada mountains while I struck out into the unknown—were all on the other side of the state, praying for me and excited for my adventure. But I was awash with guilt.

Should I be home sharing the load? Helping with our special needs son? Focusing on our family instead of this whimsical dream of writing?

After years ... no, *decades* ... of practice battling the constant threat of consuming guilt, I wielded my best weapon — prayer — and a Scripture suddenly flew into my mind:

> The purposes of a person's heart are deep waters, but one who has insight draws them out. (Proverbs 20:5, NIV)

Of course I should be here. Hadn't my husband and I talked about it for months? Prayed over the decision? Tested the sense of calling? Sought wise council? Searched Scripture?

Funny how easy it is to see God's provision and calling and purpose in another, yet doubt it unendingly in your own life. But the facts were there ... God *had* provided: the funding, the support, the time, the opportunity. He *had* called and confirmed my desire to write. Again and again and again. He *had* saturated Scripture with reminders that all His children have been instilled with purpose and seasons in which to pursue those purposes.

Writing *was* my current calling. My very soul knew it. And the season to pursue it was now.

I slipped the key from the ignition and gathered my registration documents. In the administration building, at what looked more like an upscale hotel registration desk than a Christian camp, I signed in and received a hearty welcome, a stack of maps and schedules, and the key to my room.

As I walked across the campus toward my lodging, I stopped for a moment on the edge of a large open space between buildings. It was clearly the hub of the conference, and people were streaming in from all directions. Wanting to soak in the scene, I chose a bench on the edge of the fray and watched it all unfold.

It was a little like an outdoor version of an airport arrival lounge. Friends ran to each other, hugging in greeting. Hands were shaken, faces beamed, and squeals of joy and laughter rippled everywhere. Some small groups were even praying.

From a building on my left, a door opened and people began to stream out. After a moment, I recognized many of their faces: top editors, agents, publishers, and award-winning authors. The faculty I'd come to learn from. Share my dreams with.

My heart began to pound, and doubt crept in again.

But then the faculty dispersed into the crowd until I couldn't distinguish them from the general attendees. It was just one large gathering of smiling, laughing,

My People

connected people. People who loved Jesus ... and loved writing. People who were there to pursue and explore their own callings and purposes.

People just like me.

"Your first time?" a woman with a darling pixie-cut asked as she joined me on my bench.

"How did you guess?" I replied, returning her smile.

She looked out over the mingling crowd and then turned back to me.

"Because you're glowing," she said, then her smile widened. "Welcome to the tribe."

– 14 –

Saving Nineveh

Damon J. Gray

Rabbit-hole Christians. We are rabbit-hole Christians poking our heads out of our protective havens. When the time is right, we dash from the security of our rabbit hole to the safety of another, untainted by the sin and filth of the world around us.

> Now the word of the LORD came to Jonah the son of Amittai, saying, 'Arise, go to Nineveh, that great city, and call out against it, for their evil has come up before me.' But Jonah rose to flee to Tarshish from the presence of the LORD.' (Jonah 1:1-3a, ESV)

Jonah was a faithful prophet of God until God called him to leave the comfort of his rabbit hole, directing Jonah to do something Jonah did not want to do. The underlying reasons for Jonah's hesitancy weren't relevant. The only relevant issue was that God said, "Go."

Nineveh was the infamous capital of ancient Assyria, built by Nimrod the great-grandson of Noah, and located just 280 miles north of Babylon (modern-day Iraq) on the eastern bank of the Tigris River. So ill-reputed was Nineveh that it was known as the Robber City stemming from its well-documented practice of attacking and overrunning other kingdoms in order to enrich itself. The conquests of Nineveh's King Sennacherib are so extensive as to rival those of the Roman Caesars, with exploits extending from Assyria through Jordan and as far southwest as Egypt.

The book of Jonah opens with a conjunction, "And the word of the LORD came to Jonah ..." indicating an underlying series of historical events leading up to the story about to be told. Given that history, it is no great wonder that Jonah despised the Assyrians in general, and their capital city of Nineveh in particular. Yet God told Jonah to go, and Jonah did not go.

As it was with Jonah, so it is with us. Indignity may boil to the surface as we assess the corrupted spiritual condition of our own generation and, in our piety, we may choose to avoid its members rather than attend to them. We recoil rather than engage, deeming them unworthy of our company or our ministrations. Yet this is the very community with whom our Lord, Master, and King regularly engaged.

> While Jesus was having dinner at Matthew's house, many tax collectors and *sinners* came and ate with him and his disciples. When the Pharisees saw this, they asked his disciples, "Why does your teacher eat with tax collectors and *sinners*?" (Matthew 9:10-11, TCR/NIV; emphasis added).

Paraphrased, "Why does your teacher engage in community with the dregs of society?" The answer? Because this is the heart of our God, and out of that heart, God has placed a call upon us to touch a community from which we would rather shield ourselves. We are called to be humble enough to build community by loving the unlovely, lifting the downtrodden, regarding our neighbor as ourselves.

> He lifts the poor from the dust and the needy from the garbage dump. He sets them among

> princes, placing them in seats of honor. (1 Samuel 2:8, ESV)

It has been said that Jesus' mission was not to make good people slightly better, but rather to make dead people alive. As it was with Jesus, so it must be with us. Rather than protecting our reputation through polished theology and a respectable guest list, we are to risk appearing gauche and scandalous by engaging the wrong sort of community to the extent that the guardians of orthodoxy ask the same question of us that the Pharisees asked of Jesus, "Why do they build community with druggies, drunks, and men and women of disgrace?" It is because we are desperate to see dead people brought back to life!

> He will defend the afflicted among the people and save the children of the needy; he will crush the oppressor. (Psalm 72:4, TCR/NIV)

While some may see the outcasts and rebellious as ill-advised company and lost causes, God does not ... and we do not. We understand the heart of our shepherd as one that gives up on no one. Not one sinner is beyond the ubiquitous, loving reach of our Father. They are the very ones he seeks to protect. And where the pious tend recoil, like our God, we embrace, we love, we rescue.

> "Because of the oppression of the weak and the groaning of the needy, I will now arise," says the LORD. "I will protect them from those who malign them." (Psalm 12:5, TCR/NIV)

If we refuse to build community with the very people God arises to protect, how can we ever fulfill the calling God has placed on our lives? The reason those sitting in darkness have seen a great light (Matthew 4:16) is precisely because Jesus marched the light into that darkness rather than waiting for those in darkness to find him. Accordingly, we must run toward our Nineveh rather than away from it.

When we teach the story of Jonah to our children, we speak to them of the "great wind" that whipped up a life-threatening storm. We teach them how God prepared a "great fish" that swallowed Jonah and ultimately saved his life. But the true focus of the story is neither the storm nor the fish, but rather what God repeatedly called the "great city" (Jonah 1:2, 3:2, 4:11), the community in need.

> Then the word of the LORD came to Jonah the second time, saying, "Arise, go to Nineveh, that great city, and call out against it the message that I tell you." (Jonah 3:1-2, ESV)

Following the second directive from God, Jonah did preach to Nineveh, and, amazingly, the king called on the city to join him in wearing sackcloth and ashes in hopes that God would relent from destroying Nineveh. Jonah was incensed that the city was allowed to repent, so much so that he asked God to just kill him (Jonah 4:3) and be done with it.

In his despondency, Jonah sat east of the city, waiting to see what God would do to Nineveh. It was a hot day, so God showed compassion to Jonah by raising up a vine to provide him shade, and this vine helped assuage Jonah's foul mood. Shortly thereafter, God introduced a worm which chewed on the vine and caused it to wither. Again, Jonah was incensed and asked God to kill him and end his misery.

> But God said to Jonah, "Do you have a right to be angry about the vine?" "I do," he said. "I am angry enough to die." But the LORD said, "You have been concerned about this vine, though you did not tend it or make it grow. It sprang up overnight and died overnight. But Nineveh has more than a hundred and twenty thousand people who cannot tell their right hand from their left, and many cattle as well. Should I not be concerned about that great city?" (Jonah 4:9-11, TCR/NIV)

Nineveh was a pagan city, a cruel city, but it was a city on which God chose to have compassion. Do we fool ourselves into believing that God is not concerned with the Nineveh that is our own culture, the Nineveh that has bought the endless stream of lies of the evil one? We are called to speak into our culture just as Jonah was called to speak to Nineveh.

Why do we eat with tax gatherers and sinners? Because our Lord and King eats with them. He loves them and we are learning to love them just the same.

– 15 –

The Picture
Robynne Elizabeth Miller

The paper in my hand wavered as I took in the image. A woman, wearing a boot on one foot and a sandal on the other, was centered in a pool of whiteness. Her hair was redder than mine had ever been, somewhat akin to Ronald McDonald, but her rounded cheeks, blue eyes, and stocky build were unmistakable. I was looking at a portrait of myself.

"Do you like it, Mama? Are you *especially* happy?" Noah James wondered, half questioning and half hoping. At seven, and a peculiar mix of little boy and wizened old man, he cared a great deal about making me "*especially* happy" whenever he could.

"I love it, buddy. You did a great job capturing all my best bits," I said, then paused, still looking intently at the picture. After a moment, I gave him the rest of the answer he was anxiously waiting for. "I am especially, *especially* happy about this beautiful picture."

He hugged my waist, grinned, and ran off to play.

It was clear Noah James had thought about this portrait. Besides fairly correctly rendering my hair, eye color, and undeniable roundedness, there were a lot of other me-specific details in the picture. He'd put two small, round earrings in my left ear and one in my right, for example. And there were faint brown dots across my cheeks, legs, and arms, which represented my copious amounts of freckles. The loose shirt was sage green, too. My very favorite color. There was a line on the back of my left wrist, as well, which had to be my scar from a long-ago incident involving carelessness and a very sharp knife. He'd even put me in some pedal-pushers with little ties on the cuffs like each of the three pairs I rotated through pretty much all summer long.

It gave me an odd feeling to realize he had ever really seen me … that between his obsession with books and baseball and all things Pokémon, he had quietly stored up a stash of details that somehow added up to his mother. I had, like most moms, memorized every sweet dimple and freckle on *his* little body, but it was odd to realize he had somehow done the same. He had seen me. *Seen* me.

There were some puzzling aspects to the picture, though. The strange shoe combination for one. One foot wore something like a dark brown hiking boot, and the other definitely sported a summer sandal. All my toes were present and accounted for on that foot. Each hand was outstretched and holding something, too. One of the objects was like a stick with a kind of lump on one end. A lollipop? A microphone? The other was smaller ... a lopsided square with dots all over it. I had no idea what either of them was supposed to be. I pulled the paper closer and squinted.

"Must be something awfully interesting, the way you're staring at it," a voice said. I looked up at the sound of my husband's soft, accented words. He was staying in character as a British ex-pat by making a "nice cup of tea" and grinning at me like a Cheshire cat.

"I'm trying to figure out what I'm supposed to be holding in this picture Noah James drew of me. But I seriously have no idea."

Ian came nearer and looked over my shoulder.

"The thing in your left hand is a phone. The other is a hammer." He smiled at my surprise. He wiggled his eyebrows up and down several times before confessing, "I only know that because he showed me the drawing before he gave it to you and I just asked him straight out what those things were."

I smiled back. "Did he mention why I'm holding a phone and a hammer, or why I have such interesting footwear?"

"Nope. But, then again, I didn't ask." He kissed me on the forehead, grabbed a couple of cookies to go with his tea, and went back to his office. After a few more minutes of puzzling, I got up, secured the picture with a magnet to the middle of the refrigerator door, and began to get ready for Noah James' imminent baseball game.

The next few days were a blur of activities and school events, so it wasn't until a few days later that I remembered to ask him about the picture.

"Every time I look at the fridge, I smile," I told him. "I love the way you made such an effort to draw a realistic representation of me. But I have a couple of questions … why am I wearing different shoes? And why is there a hammer in one hand and a phone in the other?"

The Picture

"Only one side of your shirt is tucked in, too," he said. As if that explained the whole thing.

"I see. So that makes three things I don't understand."

He settled in next to me on the couch and his pale forehead began to wrinkle in the way it always did when he was thinking deeply or trying to puzzle through something difficult. I ran my fingers through his sandy brown hair, flecked with copper highlights, and gave him time to gather the words he needed to explain.

"People are hard to draw," he finally said, and I nodded. The thought of trying to produce anything remotely realistic with just colored pencils and a piece of paper filled me with anxiety. But a person? That you actually knew? No thanks.

"You were especially hard," he continued, flitting his eyes up to mine as if to gauge whether this revelation upset me. I gave him a little smile but didn't know what to answer. After a moment, he continued, his voice rising slightly for emphasis. "I wanted to draw *you*, but you're not one person. I mean, you don't look like just one thing. If I drew you cooking dinner, then nobody would know you can chop wood. Or if I drew you singing on the worship team, no one would know you're good at fixing stuff. Sometimes you're out in the woodlot felling trees, and you're dirty from head to toe. But sometimes you're all dressed up and smell like soap. I couldn't think of how to draw you in a way that showed all of you. But then I had an idea …"

He slid off the couch and disappeared into the kitchen, returning with the picture in his hand. He jumped up next to me again and pointed to all the different things we'd been talking about … the shoes, the phone, the hammer.

"I thought that if I added stuff to show what you do, the picture would look more like you." He sat back and looked up at me, waiting.

"It's a brilliant idea, Noah James. Such a clever way of trying to fully convey who someone is."

His face scrunched up again, and he slowly shook his head. "I don't know. It's still not enough. I should have put in a spoon or pan or something. There's nothing in there about your cooking. And I could have put a soccer ball on the ground next to you. Or drawn a lake or something. You love the water. And there's nothing at all about singing." His lower lip trembled a little.

Wrapping him in my arms, I squeezed as hard as I could without breaking ribs. "It's perfect. We'll never be able to convey everything a person is in just one picture. Humans are a bit too complicated for that.

The Picture

But your portrait does a great job of reminding people that we're all made up of different sides and put together in complex ways. So, it's really perfect. Anyone looking at it will know that I'm someone who does, and likes, a lot of things. And maybe they'll remember that other people they know or meet are also more than what it seems on the surface."

Never one to sit still for long, he nodded as he slipped off the couch, content enough with my response, and disappeared down the hall.

That picture stayed up on the fridge for months. The reminder that people are complex and worthy to be really, especially *seen*, however, has been with me ever since.

– 16 –

We are Family
Ruth Ella Wilson

Since creation our Creator engraved His

Plan of salvation in us.

What kind of love is this?

We will never understand that

The depth, the height, and the completeness

Of our Heavenly Father's love is beyond man.

From Adam's seed came all mankind

Bearing in our bodies laminin

Ruth Ella Wilson

In the shape of the cross

That holds one cell to the next.

Love on the cross

Embedded in everybody

Reflects God's masterpiece design,

His plan of salvation for all mankind.

Because of the sorrow man caused God

In the garden, through disobedience,

Came blame and shame;

Yet, God's love remains.

Oh, Lord God, how merciful You are!

Because of His great love for fallen man

Our family grew.

Only God knew what would happen to each of you.

One family that all bleeds red blood

Needs to be covered by Jesus's blood.

Oh, Lord God, how magnificent Your plan!

The plan You have for fallen man.

Thank You, Heavenly Father, for giving humanity another chance.

We are Family

After we caused You such sorrow,

You put the rainbow in the sky

With an eternal promise to never again

Destroy the communities by flood,

Giving humanity another chance.

Oh, Lord God, how faithful You are!

Even as the years have gone by

Humanity still causes the Holy Spirit to cry.

Yet, how God demonstrates His magnificent love for us—only

His love for us nailed Jesus to the cross.

Because of Calvary hope is not lost.

Giving His beloved Son, Jesus Christ, our sovereign Savior

And keeping us from Hell's door

Causes us to love our Heavenly Father forevermore.

God is Love—and His eternal love for us

Nailed Jesus to the cross.

Because of His gift of forgiveness our Redeemer,

Jesus Christ, rose on the third day.

Now there is hope for all humanity to be set free.

Let all choose to accept the love of the cross

And reflect His light in every community.

The Love of Jesus is the vaccine our world needs.

Now, more than ever the signs are revealed

To those with eyes to see, and ears to hear

To discern that the return of our Savior is near.

Oh, Lord God, how patient You are!

Blessed are they that read and receive the truth of the redemptive story,

Ending in the Book of Revelation.

Oh, Lord God, how we look forward to being with You in glory!

– 17 –

A Woman Leave Her Home
Robynne Elizabeth Miller

Stepping into the early morning, a chilly dampness settled on my cheeks. Soft puffs of pale grey swirled along the small road and meandered passed our cottage toward the heart of our tiny rural village.

Absently pulling my collar up a little higher and plunging my gloved hands deep into my pockets, I stepped off the stone threshold, slipped through the wooden gate, and entered the lane. I was heading to a small stone church up the road.

Plodding past open fields on one side and traditional soft grey flint-stone cottages on the other, I sighed and smiled. Bowed and tilting from centuries of English weather and settling, each dwelling always seemed content and welcoming. As if a hot cup of tea and comfortable seat by the fire were waiting for you if you chanced to knock.

Close to the heart of the village, where ancient commerce once bustled, homes bore names revealing what they once were: Blacksmith's Cottage, The Malt House, Old Anchor of Hope. I cherished them all. Old. Imperfect. Beautiful.

I'd come to love this tiny hamlet and the warm, solid folks who lived in it. Even though I was six thousand miles from my original home, I was content. At least I wanted to be.

"I'm an American," I spoke into the misty morning air, as if declaring it would soothe me. But the questions still came: Could I truly be settled in any country other than the U.S.? Build a life far from my mountains and great Mexican food and people who share my tendency to laugh loudly and love fiercely?

No answer came through the fog, so I continued up the road, uncomfortable thoughts twirling and tangling in my mind.

At the grassy path leading from the street toward St. Andrew's church, I stopped and stood still, looking.

On the left was a paddock. Huge Norfolk farm horses were almost always present, regarding visitors with languid eyes and occasional slow twitches of their tails. Some plodded away in indifference, while others edged near anyone who looked suspiciously like they might be carrying an apple or sugar lump.

On the right was a tall hedge, planted to check the North Sea winds and frame the field on the other side. All English hedgerows teemed with activity and purpose: edging gardens, marking fields, providing windbreaks, sustaining animals of all kinds, and proffering deeply flavored wild fruits to those who would trouble to pluck it.

After a moment, I began again, padding through the dewy grass toward the centuries-old church nestled in a soft bend of the river ahead.

Sometimes I slipped into the musty dimness of the cool flint chapel and sang. The bare stone floors, walls, and arched ceilings provided beautiful acoustics and I'd harmonize with my own bouncing, buoyant echoes. I'd sing my fears, loneliness, dreams, and love for the God who made me, saved me, and called me to this place.

Other times, I'd sit outside on the river side of the church, quietly dreaming of all those who had come before. I would imagine the first visitors...those who had come seven centuries earlier when the church was first built. What had they worn? What did they do for work? Were they happy? Bound? Trapped?

Was I happy? Bound? Trapped?

Today was not a singing day, so I passed the tall, arched wooden doors and headed for the dew-drenched lawn.

A small bench sat near the tower and under a large weeping willow. It faced the gentle River Bure and lush, rolling farmland that, on days when mist did not obscure the view, stretched lavishly to the horizon. From this spot, with the church and village behind me, I could look out over land perfectly devoid of humans—no barns or cottages or vehicles of any kind marred the pastoral view.

The gentle gurgling of the river and quiet fluttering of willow leaves was hypnotic. The slow-swirling mist was, too, and I welcomed the sensation of calm as I sank onto the bench and into my own jumbled thoughts.

"Ya roight, there, gell?" a gruff, but kind, voice asked from somewhere behind me.

Startled, I turned and stammered, "Um, yes. Thank you, sir. I'm fine." A small, square figure stood before me, sporting a face wrinkled into folds and creases so deep I wondered how he shaved. Recovering from my surprise interruption, I smiled at having been called a "gell." Not many people were old enough to consider me a "girl."

The man rested on a long garden tool of some kind and regarded me with curious pale-grey eyes. His plain green shirt and trousers were the traditional garb of a local farm worker, but he was far too old for that now. Perhaps he now helped the parish, maintaining the churchyard? Or maybe he'd come to tend a family grave?

Adjusting his plaid cap, he leaned forward and said with a wink, "Must be somethin' loik!"

Grateful I'd lived in the village long enough to understand both his accent and his meaning, I chuckled and asked, "What 'must be something like,' sir?"

"Yer thoughts," he replied.

"I don't know if they're particularly noteworthy," I began, then impulsively added, "but they're certainly causing me a bit of grief."

"A burden shared 'tis a burden halved," he responded simply and waited.

Warmth rose in my cheeks. Why on earth had I said anything? I didn't even know what, exactly, was bothering me, let alone how to articulate it. And now a perfect stranger patiently waited for me to explain myself.

"Have you always lived here?" I asked, hoping to change the subject.

He shifted slowly, adjusting his weight carefully against his tool with a sigh. My cheeks burned even hotter as I quickly patted the empty seat next to me.

"No thanks, m'gell," he said. "If I lower meself on a damp morn' like this, I'm not loik to get back up." He then flicked his head back toward the road and the row of cottages beyond. "Last one on the end. Me gran was born there, me mum, and then meself. Me sister lives there now and I'm two cottages down. Born and bred *Narfolk* boy."

I liked the history of that. The stability and familiarity and tradition of that.

"Did you never leave?" I wondered aloud, my curiosity rising.

"Once. To serve. Stationed in Stradishall down in Suffolk. Second week there, the kitchen boiler exploded and broke me leg to bits. Was sent back home and never left again."

Never left again? I couldn't get my head round the thought of only once, for less than two weeks, being out of the county in which you were born. *Did he resent never travelling? Did he feel trapped? Angry? Shortchanged? Or did he feel deeply tethered to this place and all who'd come before?*

A Woman Leave Her Home

"Where's yer home?" I heard him ask, interrupting my racing thoughts.

"California," I answered absently, then quickly corrected myself. "I mean, here. Norfolk. The village." Unexpected tears began to brim and I pressed my lips together.

"No," he said softly. "Where's yer *home?*"

Puzzled, I searched his grizzled face. He smiled and waited, clearly expecting me to grasp his meaning.

I didn't.

After a short while, he ended the silence by changing the subject. He'd seen me come, he said. Some days, when his leg hurt, he'd sit by the window and watch what happened in the lane, so he knew I often visited the church. He liked the look of my husband and kids, too, when I brought them with me. "A nice family," he declared, "with plenty of pluck and cheek."

I laughed a little. He was right there—I had four cheeky kids, all right.

"I *hear* you, too," he said in a conspiratorial tone, pausing dramatically as my eyes grew large and profound embarrassment returned. "When I see you're alone, I watch to see if it's a *church day* or a *bench day*. If it's a church day, and me legs are workin', I grab me cap and come tend me mum and dad's graves. I like to hear you singin'."

He stopped again, grinning broadly as he shifted his weight before continuing.

"There's a sound some make which is pleasin' enough," he said, pausing to make sure I was absorbing his meaning, "but, there's others," he went on carefully, "who'er doing more than that. They're singing the songs of heaven."

My tears began to brim again as he leaned in and almost whispered with the tenderness of a father, "Where's yer *home,* m'gell?" This time, I realized he wasn't expecting an answer. And he wasn't talking about California.

I smiled at him and nodded, throat closed and unable to speak. He touched his cap and limped slowly back over the grass. When I could see him no longer, I turned back to my view, no longer obscured by clouds of swirling mist.

Index of Authors

Brundage, Randy	51
Burns, Tessa	77
Celovsky, Debra	69
Gray, Damon J.	91
Gruelle, Deb	11
Hagion, Christine	3
Hellard-Brown, Terrie	47
Hoss, Christy	39
Mackinnon, Malcolm	57
Miller, Robynne Elizabeth	85, 99, 111
Sage, Susan	25
Siden, Marilyn	19
Warren, Debbie Jones	61
Weinberg, D.H.	31
Wilson, Ruth Ella	107

Meet the Authors

Randy Brundage

Randy lives alone in the Sacramento area. He has 2 amazing sons, one awesome daughter, and a remarkable daughter-in-law. He has previously published in Inspire Kindness and Inspire Grace. He is very thankful for the opportunities that ICW has provided and hopes to someday be a real writer.

Tessa Burns

Tessa lives in Northern California with her husband and golden retriever. She is the mother of three adult children. She holds an MSN in nursing and works as a school nurse. She enjoys writing, painting, playing the piano, singing, and just about anything creative.

Debra Celovsky

Debra's work has appeared in a number of Christian publications, including the Inspire Kindness anthology. Most of her adult life has been in pastoral work with her husband. She is currently on the board of Inspire Christian Writers and blogs about family legacy at debracelovsky.com.

Damon J. Gray

Damon is a writer, speaker, husband, father, grandfather, former pastor, and member of the Inspire Board of Directors. Damon pursues his passion for teaching, making disciples, and advancing the kingdom of Jesus Christ, by calling on men and women to embrace Long-View Living in a Short-View World.

Deb Gruelle

Deb serves as Inspire's chaplain. The 2nd Edition of her book, Aching for a Child: Emotional, Spiritual, and Ethical Insights for Women Struggling with Infertility and Miscarriage, releases in in October 2021. She's the bestselling author of two children's books, with a third, Ten Little Fireflies, releasing in March 2022.

Christine Hagion

Christine previously worked at Valley Medical Center, a hospital with a level-1 trauma unit and a rehabilitation department renowned for advances in treating traumatic brain injury. While at the Rehabilitation Research Center, Christine edited the Essential Brain Injury Guide, the manual required in preparation for the national certification exam.

Meet the Authors

Terrie Hellard-Brown

Terrie writes devotionals and children's stories. Her podcast, Books that Spark, reviews books that lead to teachable moments with our kids. Her blog discusses being Christ's disciple while discipling our children. Terrie uses her experiences as a mother, missionary, minister, and teacher to speak to the hearts of readers.

Christy Hoss

Christy is the author of The Rubber Band Middle Grade novel series. She is a freelance editor for Elk Lake Publishing Inc. She writes children's Bible stories for Focus on the Family ClubHouse magazine and has written articles for Guideposts. She is a featured speaker for conferences, retreats and special events. Christy lives in Northern California with Kevin, the love of her life. They have three grown children.

Malcolm Mackinnon

Malcolm, originally from England, has been a resident of the Bay Area since 2011. Married to Donna with two beautiful adopted children, he's a children's pastor, having previously worked as a portrait artist, painter, proofreader, pastor... in fact, anything that starts with 'P.' He's looking forward to being a pirate!

Robynne Elizabeth Miller

Robynne holds a B.A. in English Literature and an MFA in Creative Nonfiction and Fiction. Ten books, multiple anthologies, several collaborations, and countless articles/essays into her career, she's a writing and publishing coach, substantive editor, ongoing mentor and Inspire's president. Her passion is equipping writers to succeed.

Susan Sage

Susan loves to write flash fiction and devotionals. She is also a teacher, mentor, speaker, and loves praying and encouraging others in their walk with God. Susan and her husband make their home in beautiful N. Idaho. She is the critique group leader facilitator and PR director for Inspire.

Marilyn Siden

Marilyn has published two books--Potholes in the Pavement and Finding Common Ground. She directed camping ministries for battered children for thirty-five years. She has a deep love of music, little plants that bloom in impossible places, anything in the out-of-doors, occasional backpacking, swimming, reading, and pelicans.

Debbie Jones Warren

Born in Alameda, Debbie moved to Nigeria with her missionary parents before her first birthday. Now in Castro Valley, she and her husband, Chris, love time with their three adult children and their oldest son's wife. Debbie enjoys cooking gluten-free, learning German, and hosting backyard teas for friends.

D.H. Weinberg

D.H. is a writer of suspense thrillers, historical fiction, and inspirational literature. After a career in business, he has devoted himself to writing full time. He lives in Southern California with his wife and 7 year old golden retriever, Kona, and is a foodie, explorer, and adventurer.

Ruth Ella Wilson

Ruth is the author of the Love Beyond Borders four-book series written for children to teach spiritual truths in an engaging, culturally-competent way. Ruth Ella Wilson (author's pen name) honors her loved ones. Her mother's name is Ruth, her grandmother's is Ella, and Wilson is from her father's lineage.

About Inspire Christian Writers

Inspire Christian Writers is a nonprofit organization whose sole reason for existing is to equip and encourage writers, no matter where you are in your writing career. Started in California, Inspire now has members from multiple countries and across the US. And what was begun as a simple writing group has developed into a comprehensive organization meeting the needs of writers in numerous ways:

- Our award-winning blog and website, (named a top ten world-wide resource for Christian writers!)
- Online and in-person critique groups
- Writing Contests
- Directory of vetted professionals serving writers
- Workshops, both in-person and online
- Bi-annual Summer Symposium
- Networking opportunities
- Annual anthology
- Discounts for members
- And the Inspire Christian Writers conference at Mt. Hermon

Inspire Community

If you are interested in joining Inspire, or want information on our current events and offerings, please go to www.inspirewriters.com.

We look forward to welcoming you into our family!

Previous Anthologies from Inspire Christian Writers

Inspire Trust (2012)

Inspire Faith (2013)

Friends of Inspire Faith (2013)

Inspired Glimpses of God's Presence (2013)

Inspire Victory (2014)

Inspire Promise (2014)

Inspire Forgiveness (2015)

Inspire Joy (2016)

Inspire Love (2017)

Inspire Kindness (2018)

Inspire Grace (2019)

Made in the USA
Coppell, TX
06 June 2022